TO:

_____

FROM:

_____

BEDTIME BLESSINGS & PRAYERS FOR BRAVE BOYS

Glenn Hascall

BEDTIME
BLESSINGS
& PRAYERS
FOR
BRAVE
BOYS

Read-Aloud Devotions

BARBOUR **kidz**
A Division of Barbour Publishing

Member of the
Evangelical Christian
Publishers Association

Printed in China.

001032 0222 HA

CONTENTS

I WILL LIE DOWN
AND SLEEP IN PEACE.
O LORD, YOU ALONE
KEEP ME SAFE.

PSALM 4:8

INTRODUCTION

*"The eyes of the Lord move over all the
earth so that He may give strength to those
whose whole heart is given to Him."*
2 CHRONICLES 16:9

God is looking for brave boys who want to live for Him.
Is that you? Maybe you don't always feel brave. These
short devotions have been written to help you grow
braver and stronger. When you give your life to Jesus
and His Holy Spirit comes to live inside you, He will
make you brave. And as you read God's words in the
Bible and pray, you will have more of God's power to
make you strong. So let's get going and show God and
others that you want to be brave for Him!

BLESSING #1:
YOU ARE LOVED

TONIGHT your head will sink into your pillow. When your eyes close in sleep, there is one thing you need to remember—God loves you. He always has, you know. And He always will.

God takes care of everything while you sleep. This means you never have to worry about anything. God isn't afraid of the dark. When you need Him to help, He will help. God is love, and He loves you. In fact, He thought love was such a good idea that He made it His most important rule.

I AM LOVED BY YOU, GOD. HELP ME LOVE OTHERS.

Jesus said. . ."You must love the Lord your God with all your heart and with all your soul and with all your mind."

MATTHEW 22:37

BLESSING #2:
YOU ARE FORGIVEN

WHEN you do something you know you shouldn't do, you might feel bad. You might be afraid someone will find out. You might want to hide. Maybe you feel this way right now.

God wants you to tell Him what you've done. This is a way you can let Him know "You were right, and I was wrong." This is when you tell God you're sorry. And forgiveness is what you need.

Before you go to sleep tonight, pray. Tell God about all the things you are sorry for. He listens. He forgives.

**I CAN CHOOSE TO OBEY YOU
AND DO THE RIGHT THING, GOD.
HELP ME MAKE GOOD CHOICES.**

*If we tell [God] our sins, He is faithful and
we can depend on Him to forgive us.*
1 JOHN 1:9

BLESSING #3:
YOU ARE ONE OF A KIND

WHEN God creates, it isn't like in a toy factory where every toy is made with the same parts and put together in exactly the same way. When God made you, He made every part of you to fit just right. No one is exactly like you. And no one can do all the things God made you to do.

You are special to God. You are part of His good plans. His plans are perfect!

Tell Him, "Thanks!"

YOU DIDN'T MAKE ME LOOK, SOUND, AND ACT LIKE OTHER BOYS, GOD. I CAN ACT MORE LIKE YOU BECAUSE YOU MADE ME TO BE LIKE YOU.

You made the parts inside me.
You put me together inside my mother.
PSALM 139:13

BLESSING #4:
YOU ARE GIFTED

GOD made you, and He made you to do something special. He knows you will be very good at it too!

You might have heard someone say that a person is "gifted." This means a person can do something well because God gave them the ability to do it.

When you use your God-given gift, it can be used to help others.

Tonight, dream big dreams about how you can help other boys and girls.

I LEARN MORE EVERY DAY, GOD. TEACH ME HOW TO FOLLOW WHERE YOU LEAD ME. HELP ME DO WHAT YOU MADE ME TO DO.

God has given each of you a gift.
Use it to help each other.
1 PETER 4:10

WHEN you have a reason for doing something, it's called "purpose." It's sad when a person can't find a reason to do something good.

The most important reason to always do your best is God—because You work for Him. His plan was to give you a reason to do the right thing. God helps you and is always there for you. He will *always* show you the right thing to do. With His help, you can do it!

I CAN MAKE THE GOOD CHOICE TO OBEY YOU, GOD. YOUR LOVE IS THE BEST REASON TO SPEND TIME DOING WHAT YOU KNOW I CAN DO.

We can work for [God].
He planned that we should do this.
EPHESIANS 2:10

DO you feel strong? Have you ever flexed your muscles and smiled, thinking about how strong you will be when you're all grown up?

God helps His kids. He is strong when they are weak. He can even make them stronger. He never leaves His kids alone. And because God is with you, that makes *you* strong!

When you're afraid, it's easy to forget that God is strong. But don't forget. Don't lose hope. Don't hide. This is a time to smile, because God is with you. He loves you, and He can—and *will!*—make you strong.

THANKS FOR BEING STRONG WHEN I SLEEP, GOD. AND THANKS FOR MAKING ME STRONG WHEN I WAKE UP EACH MORNING.

"Be strong and have strength of heart! . . . For the Lord your God is with you anywhere you go."
JOSHUA 1:9

BLESSING #7:
YOU ARE
CHOSEN

WHEN kids choose teams on the playground, the chosen ones can either choose to join the team or walk away. It's just like that with God. He chose you, but you have to make a choice. You can stay and follow Him, or you can walk away.

When you join God's team, you get to work with other Christians and do work that is super important to God.

God never wondered if He loved You enough before He chose you. He loves you. *Never forget that!* And He chose you. *Always remember that!*

THANK YOU FOR CHOOSING ME, GOD. I WILL FOLLOW YOU.

God loves you and. . .He has chosen you.
1 Thessalonians 1:4

BLESSING #8:
YOU ARE PROTECTED

LULLABIES are simple songs that calm you and help you fall sleep. You can make up your own lullabies. Sing calming songs about God and how He protects you. Sing songs of thanks to Him. These songs will remind you that you never have to be afraid. They can help you trust God, who has never stopped loving you.

No matter what happens, day or night, God is with you. His protection is better than anything else. Sing a song. Say good night!

**I AM PROTECTED WHEN I CLOSE
MY EYES, GOD. YOU KEEP ME SAFE.
YOU ALWAYS HAVE, AND YOU ALWAYS WILL.**

You keep me safe from trouble.
PSALM 32:7

BLESSING #9:
YOU ARE SPECIAL

GOD calls you a "masterpiece." This means you are one of a kind and very special to Him. When you comb your hair, remember that God made your hair and knows how many hairs you have—whether it's a little or a lot! He gave you hands so they could be held. He gave you something to say and words to speak so you can tell others what you're thinking. God accepts you and calls you His child. He loves you!

YOU ARE IMPORTANT TO ME, GOD.
AND YOU SAY I AM IMPORTANT TO YOU.
HELP ME TO BELIEVE IT AND
THEN CELEBRATE!

"You are of great worth in My eyes."
Isaiah 43:4

YOU have ideas, and some of them are really good! But some of your ideas will fail, and even that is a good thing. Because when things fail, you're learning what doesn't work. So keep thinking. Keep dreaming. God loves your good ideas.

God can help you. His strength makes you brave. Your bravery helps you try new things. And when you try, you are trusting God. That's how amazing things get done.

I WILL KEEP TRYING IF YOU WILL KEEP HELPING ME, GOD. YOUR STRENGTH HELPS ME TO BE BRAVE ENOUGH TO CREATE NEW THINGS.

I can do all things because
Christ gives me the strength.
PHILIPPIANS 4:13

BLESSING #11:
YOU ARE A LEADER

GOD leads. You follow. This is a good way to do things, because God knows more than you do—He knows *everything*! He can teach you. Then He will let you lead others. It's important to remember that good leaders aren't bossy. They show others the right way to do things. When people see you do the right thing, they can follow your example.

Leaders help others. They don't wait for someone else to do the hard work. Tomorrow ask your mom or dad if there is anything you can do to help them out. Be a leader!

I WANT TO BE A LEADER.
HELP ME LEARN FROM YOU, GOD.

"Do for other people what you would like to have them do for you."

Luke 6:31

BLESSING #12:
YOU ARE FREE

THERE are rules you need to follow at home:

Brush your teeth.

Make your bed.

Eat your dinner before dessert.

But. . .the Bible says you are "free." So, does that mean it's okay if you break the rules? No! God made you free to *follow* the rules.

This kind of freedom is a very special gift from God. And this special gift belongs to YOU!

I DON'T HAVE TO FOLLOW KIDS WHO BREAK THE RULES, GOD. WHEN I BREAK THE RULES, I GET IN TROUBLE. HELP ME TO BE A RULE FOLLOWER.

"If the Son makes you free,
you will be free for sure."
JOHN 8:36

BLESSING #13:
YOU CAN READ
GOD'S WORD

YOU might be reading these words all by yourself right now. Or maybe someone is reading them to you. Now, think about reading your Bible. All the words in the Bible are what God wants to say to you. You can learn from every word and know it's all true. God wrote it, and He can't lie.

God's Word can help you understand things better and learn things you didn't know before. It's like a flashlight in the darkness that can help you see where you're going so you don't trip over something in your path.

YOUR WORD WAS WRITTEN FOR
ME, GOD. EVERY WORD MEANS
SOMETHING SPECIAL. EXPLORING
THE BIBLE IS LIKE A TREASURE HUNT.

Your Word is a lamp to my feet
and a light to my path.
PSALM 119:105

BLESSING #14:
YOU CAN TALK TO GOD

GOD is always close. He is with you wherever you go. He is the best friend you could ever have. But how can you *talk* to God?

Brave boys pray. They don't use a cell phone or video chat.

You might be under your comfy covers right now. Maybe you're tucked in for the night. Pray right where you are. When you pray, you have *all* of God's attention.

THANKS FOR STANDING BESIDE ME, GOD.
WHEN I HAVE A BAD DAY, IT'S GOOD
TO KNOW I DON'T HAVE TO TRY TO
FIGURE THINGS OUT ON MY OWN,
BECAUSE YOU ARE WITH ME.

The Lord is near to all who call on Him,
to all who call on Him in truth.
PSALM 145:18

WHEN bad things happen to the bravest boys, they can still be joyful.

Did you know that *happy* and *joyful* are different things? When you are happy, it's because something good happened. When you are joyful, it means you believe God is taking care of everything—even the bad things.

You have every reason to be joyful. It means you are learning enough about God to know that He can take bad things and somehow make them good.

I DON'T NEED TO STAY SAD WHEN
BAD THINGS HAPPEN, GOD. HELP ME
REMEMBER THAT YOU CAN CHANGE
WHAT I THOUGHT WAS A SAD ENDING
INTO A VERY GOOD ONE.

Be full of joy always because you belong to the Lord.
PHILIPPIANS 4:4

BLESSING #16:
YOU HAVE HOPE

YOU might hope you get a gift when a family member comes for a visit. This hope is often called a wish. It's why some people throw coins in a fountain or look into the sky for a special star. They don't really know if what they want will happen, but they make a wish just in case.

When God talks about hope, He means something very different. To God, hope is not a wish but something you *believe* will happen. Be brave. Have hope. Believe God will do what He says.

YOU GIVE ME HOPE AS I FOLLOW YOU, GOD. MAKE MY HOPE STRONGER AND STRONGER.

Hope comes from God. . . . May your hope grow stronger by the power of the Holy Spirit.
ROMANS 15:13

BLESSING #17:
YOU CAN ENJOY GOD'S CREATION

GOD used water to carve canyons, soil to grow flowers, and the moon to bring a little light to a dark night. He wants you to enjoy *all* of His creation.

In the morning, you can see the sun, trees, and all kinds of beautiful things. The sunset will show up tomorrow night, and it will look different than it did tonight.

Lots of animals live outside, and God made them too. God even feeds them and gives them water to drink.

GOD, YOUR CREATION IS BEAUTIFUL. AND I AM SO THANKFUL I GET TO ENJOY ALL OF IT.

[God] made all things. Nothing was made without Him making it.

JOHN 1:3

BLESSING #18:
YOU HAVE CHOICES

YOU could look for treasure anywhere other than God, but that would be foolish. His gift of wisdom is a treasure. God says wisdom is worth more than gold. You might think of all the things you could buy with treasure. But God's wisdom is better because it lasts forever, and it never needs to be returned and never wears out.

What's your choice, brave boy—gold or wisdom? Choose wisdom. Then you'll learn how to make good choices for life!

IT'S IMPOSSIBLE TO FOLLOW TWO LEADERS, GOD. HELP ME FOLLOW YOU AND ACCEPT THE GIFTS YOU OFFER. WHAT A GREAT CHOICE!

To get wisdom is much better than getting gold.
PROVERBS 16:16

LIFE can be hard. God understands. You can be happy one moment and sad the next. God understands. You can make good choices and bad choices on the same day. God understands.

You can't be strong without God's help. You can't make good choices without His wisdom. And you can't save yourself. He knows the choices you will make, and He stands ready to cheer on the good and rescue you from the bad.

I AM ASKING FOR YOUR HELP, GOD. BEING BRAVE SOMETIMES MEANS ASKING FOR HELP BECAUSE YOU UNDERSTAND ME.

[Jesus] understands how weak we are.
Hebrews 4:15

YOU can't keep a secret from God. No one knows you better than He does. He knows what your favorite things are. He knows what you want to do when you grow up. He knows what makes you angry. He even knows who your best friends are.

When you pray, it's not helpful to keep anything from God. He already knows everything anyway. God wants to see if you'll share everything with Him—even your biggest secrets. So talk to Him right now. Tell Him everything, brave boy.

WHEN I PRAY, I AM TALKING TO YOU, GOD. HELP ME TO BE HONEST. I WANT YOUR LOVE TO KEEP CHANGING ME FOR GOOD.

O Lord, You have looked through me
and have known me.
Psalm 139:1

LIFE can be very busy. Sometimes it's hard to get everything done. When you're so busy, it's hard to find time to rest. You spend a lot of time in a vehicle going from one important thing to the next. Sometimes you're so tired that you fall asleep on the way to your next activity.

You need rest. It's a chance for you to stop and think about what God has done and is doing for you. It's like a cold drink of water on a hot day—it's refreshing and helps you feel better. God can help you rest.

I GET SO TIRED, GOD. HELP ME LEARN HOW TO GET GOOD REST. TEACH ME.

"Come to Me, all of you who work and have heavy loads. I will give you rest."
MATTHEW 11:28

BLESSING #22:
YOU CAN PLAY

YOU might be surprised that there is a verse in the Bible about boys and girls playing in the streets. God wants you to play and have fun. Play is a good way for you to get exercise and stay healthy.

God made the outdoors for human beings to enjoy. When you play outside, you can make new friends and discover new and interesting things about nature. Do you think God is pleased when you enjoy His creation?

I CAN ENJOY PLAYING OUTSIDE, BECAUSE YOU MADE EVERYTHING I NEED FOR PLAYING. THANK YOU, GOD.

"The city will be filled with boys and girls playing in the streets."

ZECHARIAH 8:5

BLESSING #23:
YOU CAN LAUGH

IF God didn't want you to laugh, then it would seem like He didn't want you to enjoy life. But that's not true. God *does* want you to laugh and have fun!

God's Word says that there is a right time to feel certain ways and a right time to do certain things. It is right to cry when something is sad; and it is right to laugh when you are happy.

SOMETIMES JOY CAN MAKE ME
LAUGH, GOD. THE SOUND OF MY
LAUGH MIGHT BRING JOY TO YOU
ALSO. THANK YOU FOR LAUGHTER.

There is a time to cry, and a time to laugh.
ECCLESIASTES 3:4

BLESSING #24:
YOU CAN LEARN

YOU have learned so much since the day you were born. You are learning more every day. Tomorrow you will learn something new. And learning new things is a reason to celebrate!

Before you go to sleep tonight, think of all the things you've learned so far. Make a list! Then make another list of all the things you *want* to learn.

God can teach you when you're willing to learn new things!

YOU HAVE SO MANY THINGS TO TEACH ME, GOD. HELP ME BE WILLING TO LEARN. HELP ME BE WILLING TO DO WHAT YOU ASK ME TO DO.

Teach a man who is right and good,
and he will grow in learning.
PROVERBS 9:9

BLESSING #25:
YOU WERE CREATED BY GOD

YOU are not a mistake. God knew your name even before you were born. God is powerful enough to create life, and He chose to give you life, brave boy! You were made in His image—this means you were made to look and act like Him.

To God, you're not a science experiment; you're a part of His family. He gave you a mind and heart. He gave you a soul and spirit. He asks you to walk with Him. Walking with God helps give a purpose—a reason—for everything you do.

YOU GIVE ME YOUR BEST, GOD. YOU NEVER GIVE UP ON ME. THANK YOU.

Then God said, "Let Us make man like Us."
GENESIS 1:26

DID you know that there's a place where no one gets hurt or makes bad choices? A place where no one dies and you get to see God? It's hard to imagine, but God made the promise of heaven. And God *always* keeps His promises.

Heaven is real! And if you know God and have asked Him into your heart, you'll get to go there one day. God will have everything ready for you, and there will be a celebration when you arrive.

Sleep well tonight, knowing that because of Jesus, today, tomorrow, and every day after that is going to be amazing!

HEAVEN IS A PLACE THAT I CAN'T WAIT TO SEE, GOD. HEAVEN IS MY REAL HOME!

[Jesus said,] "There are many rooms in My Father's house. . . . I am going away to make a place for you."
JOHN 14:2

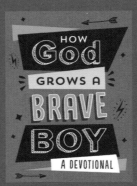